DISNEP
PRESENTS

THE LION KING

Music & Lyrics by
ELTON JOHN & TIM RICE

Additional Music & Lyrics by
LEBO M, MARK MANCINA, JAY RIFKIN, JULIE TAYMOR, HANS ZIMMER

Book by
ROGER ALLERS & IRENE MECCHI

Starring

JOHN VICKERY   SAMUEL E. WRIGHT

GEOFF HOYLE   TSIDII LE LOKA   TOM ALAN ROBBINS

JASON RAIZE   HEATHER HEADLEY

STANLEY WAYNE MATHIS   TRACY NICOLE CHAPMAN   KEVIN CAHOON

SCOTT IRBY-RANNIAR   KAJUANA SHUFORD
and
MAX CASELLA

KEVIN BAILEY   EUGENE BARRY-HILL   GINA BREEDLOVE   CAMILLE M. BROWN   IRESOL CARDONA
ALBERTO CRUZ, Jr.   MARK ALLAN DAVIS   LINDIWE DLAMINI   NTOMB'KHONA DLAMINI   SHEILA GIBBS
LANA GORDON   LINDIWE HLENGWA   TIMOTHY HUNTER   CHRISTOPHER JACKSON   JENNIFER JOSEPHS
VANESSA A. JONES   MICHAEL JOY   FACA KULU   RON KUNENE   SONYA LESLIE   AUBREY LYNCH II
PHILIP DORIAN McADOO   SAM McKELTON   PETER ANTHONY MOORE   NANDI MORAKE   NHLANHLA NGEMA
KARINE PLANTADIT-BAGEOT   DANNY RUTIGLIANO   LEVENSKY SMITH   ASHI K. SMYTHE
ENDALYN TAYLOR-SHELLMAN   RACHEL TECORA TUCKER   FRANK WRIGHT II   CHRISTINE YASUNAGA   and LEBO M

Adapted from the screenplay by
IRENE MECCHI & JONATHAN ROBERTS & LINDA WOOLVERTON

Produced by
PETER SCHNEIDER & THOMAS SCHUMACHER

Scenic Design	*Costume Design*	*Lighting Design*	*Mask & Puppet Design*
RICHARD HUDSON	JULIE TAYMOR	DONALD HOLDER	JULIE TAYMOR & MICHAEL CURRY

Sound Design	*Hair & Makeup Design*	*Casting*
TONY MEOLA	MICHAEL WARD	JAY BINDER

Technical Director	*Production Stage Manager*	*Press Representative*
DAVID BENKEN	JEFF LEE	BONEAU/BRYAN-BROWN

Music Director	*Orchestrators*	*Music Coordinator*
JOSEPH CHURCH	ROBERT ELHAI DAVID METZGER BRUCE FOWLER	MICHAEL KELLER

Music Produced for the Stage & Additional Score by
MARK MANCINA

Associate Music Producer
ROBERT ELHAI

Additional Vocal Score, Vocal Arrangements & Choral Director
LEBO M

Choreography by
GARTH FAGAN

Directed by
JULIE TAYMOR

SCENES AND MUSICAL NUMBERS
ACT ONE

Scene 1	Pride Rock
	"Circle of Life" . . . . .Rafiki, Ensemble
Scene 2	Scar's Cave
Scene 3	Rafiki's Tree
Scene 4	The Pridelands
	"The Morning Report" .Zazu, Young Simba, Mufasa
Scene 5	Scar's Cave
Scene 6	The Pridelands
	"I Just Can't Wait to be King" . . . . . . .Young Simba, Young Nala, Zazu, Ensemble
Scene 7	Elephant Graveyard
	"Chow Down" . . . . .Shenzi, Banzai, Ed
Scene 8	Under the Stars
	"They Live in You" . . . . .Mufasa, Ensemble
Scene 9	Elephant Graveyard
	"Be Prepared" .Scar, Shenzi, Banzai, Ed, Ensemble
Scene 10	The Gorge
Scene 11	Pride Rock
	"Be Prepared" (Reprise) . . . . Scar, Ensemble
Scene 12	Rafiki's Tree
Scene 13	The Desert/The Jungle
	"Hakuna Matata" . . . . .Timon, Pumbaa, Young Simba, Simba, Ensemble

ACT TWO

Entr'acte	"One by One". . . . . Ensemble
Scene 1	Scar's Cave
	"The Madness of King Scar" . . . . .Scar, Zazu, Banzai, Shenzi, Ed, Nala
Scene 2	The Pridelands
	"Shadowland" . . . . .Nala, Rafiki, Ensemble
Scene 3	The Jungle
Scene 4	Under the Stars
	"Endless Night" . . . . .Simba, Ensemble
Scene 5	Rafiki's Tree
Scene 6	The Jungle
	"Can You Feel the Love Tonight" . . . . . .Timon, Pumbaa, Simba, Nala, Ensemble
	"He Lives in You" (Reprise) . . . . .Rafiki, Simba, Ensemble
Scene 7	Pride Rock
	"King of Pride Rock"/"Circle of Life" (Reprise) . . . . .Ensemble

THERE WILL BE ONE FIFTEEN-MINUTE INTERMISSION

SONG CREDITS

All songs by Elton John (music) and Tim Rice (lyrics) except as follows:
"He Lives in You" ("They Live in You"): Music and lyrics by Mark Mancina, Jay Rifkin, and Lebo M;
"One by One": Music and lyrics by Lebo M; **"Shadowland"**: Music by Hans Zimmer and Lebo M,
lyrics by Mark Mancina and Lebo M; **"Endless Night"**: Music by Lebo M, Hans Zimmer, and Jay Rifkin,
lyrics by Julie Taymor; **"King of Pride Rock"**: Music by Hans Zimmer, lyrics by Lebo M

ADDITIONAL SCORE
Grasslands chant and Lioness chant by Lebo M; Rafiki's chants by Tsidii Le Loka

CAST IN ORDER OF APPEARANCE

RAFIKI . . . . .Tsidii Le Loka
MUFASA . . . . Samuel E. Wright
SARABI . . . . Gina Breedlove
ZAZU . . . . Geoff Hoyle
SCAR . . . . John Vickery
YOUNG SIMBA . . . . Scott Irby-Ranniar
YOUNG NALA . . . . Kajuana Shuford
SHENZI . . . . .Tracy Nicole Chapman
BANZAI . . . . Stanley Wayne Mathis
ED . . . . Kevin Cahoon
TIMON . . . . Max Casella
PUMBAA . . . . Tom Alan Robbins
SIMBA . . . . Jason Raize
NALA . . . . Heather Headley
ENSEMBLE SINGERS . . Eugene Barry-Hill, Gina Breedlove, Ntomb'khona Dlamini,
Sheila Gibbs, Lindiwe Hlengwa, Christopher Jackson,
Vanessa A. Jones, Faca Kulu, Ron Kunene, Philip Dorian McAdoo,
Sam McKelton, Lebo M, Nandi Morake
ENSEMBLE DANCERS . . . Camille M. Brown, Iresol Cardona, Mark Allan Davis,
Lana Gordon, Timothy Hunter, Michael Joy, Aubrey Lynch II,
Karine Plantadit-Bageot, Endalyn Taylor-Shellman,
Levensky Smith, Ashi K. Smythe, Christine Yasunaga

SWINGS AND UNDERSTUDIES

(Understudies never substitute for listed players unless announced at the time of the performance.)
RAFIKI: Sheila Gibbs, Lindiwe Hlengwa; MUFASA: Eugene Barry-Hill, Philip Dorian McAdoo;
SARABI: Camille M. Brown, Vanessa A. Jones; ZAZU: Kevin Cahoon, Danny Rutigliano; SCAR:
Kevin Bailey; YOUNG SIMBA: Alberto Cruz, Jr.; YOUNG NALA: Jennifer Josephs; SHENZI:
Lana Gordon, Vanessa A. Jones; BANZAI: Philip Dorian McAdoo, Levensky Smith; ED: Frank
Wright II; TIMON: Kevin Cahoon, Danny Rutigliano; PUMBAA: Philip Dorian McAdoo, Danny
Rutigliano; SIMBA: Timothy Hunter, Christopher Jackson; NALA: Lindiwe Hlengwa, Sonya Leslie

SWINGS: Lindiwe Dlamini, Sonya Leslie, Peter Anthony Moore, Nhlanhla Ngema,
Rachel Tecora Tucker, Frank Wright II

Lindiwe Dlamini, Ntomb'khona Dlamini, Lindiwe Hlengwa, Faca Kulu, Tsidii Le Loka, and Nhlanhla
Ngema are appearing with the permission of **Actors' Equity Association**

ORCHESTRA
Conductor–Joseph Church
Associate Conductor: Karl Jurman; *Wood Flute Soloist/Flute/Piccolo:* David Weiss; *Concertmistress:*
Claudia Hafer-Tondi; *Violins:* Francisca Mendoza, Avril Brown; *Violin/Viola:* Ralph Farris; *Cellos:*
Eliana Mendoza, Bruce Wang; *Flute/Clarinet/Bass Clarinet:* Bob Keller; *French Horns:* Kait
Mahony, Jeff Scott; *Trombone:* Rock Ciccarone; *Bass Trombone/Tuba:* George Flynn; *Upright &
Electric Basses:* Luico Hopper; *Drums:* Tommy Igoe; *Guitar:* Kevin Kuhn; *Mallets/Percussion:*
Valerie Dee Naranjo, Tom Brett; *Percussion:* Junior "Gabu" Wedderburn, Rolando Morales-Matos;
Keyboard Synthesizers: Ted Baker, Karl Jurman, Cynthia Kortman
Music Coordinator–Michael Keller

Based on the Disney film

THE
LION KING

Directed by Roger Allers and Rob Minkoff
Produced by Don Hahn

**Special thanks to all the artists and staff of
Walt Disney Feature Animation**

PROFILES

JOHN VICKERY (*Scar*) Broadway: *The Sisters Rosensweig, The Real Thing, Eminent Domain, Ned & Jack,* and *Macbeth* (Lincoln Center). Regional/Off-Broadway appearances, too numerous to list exhaustively, include the title roles in *Tartuffe, Don Juan, The Misanthrope, Hamlet, Macbeth, Richard II, Richard III, Pericles, The Death of von Richthofen,* and *Romeo and Juliet.* Film: *Patriot Games, Big Business, Dr. Giggles, Rapid Fire,* and *Out of Bounds.* He dedicates his performance to Alexandria Grace.

SAMUEL E. WRIGHT (*Mufasa*) has appeared on Broadway in *Promises, Promises, Jesus Christ Superstar, Two Gentlemen of Verona, Pippin, Over Here,* Cy Coleman's *Welcome to the Club, Mule Bone,* and *The Tap Dance Kid* (Tony nomination). Mr. Wright portrayed Dizzy Gillespie in *Bird,* and Sebastian the calypso crab in Disney's *The Little Mermaid* (his song "Under the Sea" won an Oscar). His Disney album, *Sebastian,* has been RIAA Certified Gold.

GEOFF HOYLE (*Zazu*) Clowned with Pickle Family Circus, Cirque du Soleil, Circus Flora. Wrote and performed solo award-winning stage shows— *Boomer!, Feast of Fools, The Convict's Return, Geoff Hoyle: The First Hundred Years*—in New York, San Francisco, London, Paris, and Russia. Has received five NEA grants. Numerous comic stage performances at Berkeley Rep, ACT, ART, Arena Stage, La Jolla Playhouse. This one's for Jonah, Daniel, and Kailey.

TSIDII LE LOKA (*Rafiki*), a South African vocalist/songwriter, has performed with Miriam Makeba, Max Roach, and Harry Belafonte. Television: "Tsidii Le Loka in Concert" (South Africa) and "Caught in the Act" (USA/1995 Iris Award); numerous commercials and endorsements (Johnson & Johnson). Recordings: Blue Note Records' "When Doves Cry" and Yal Records' "Heart Vision" by Yusef Lateef. Tsidii holds two Bachelor degrees in Economics and Music (University of Massachusetts, Amherst/Berklee College).

MAX CASELLA (*Timon*) returns to New York and makes his Broadway debut. Best known to audiences around the world as "Vinnie," the quirky, charming best friend of "Doogie Howser, M.D.," Max has starred in films from *Ed Wood* to *Sgt. Bilko.* He has been on stage from Boston to Los Angeles, and when not acting, is developing and writing a screenplay based on a John Fante novel. Hakuna Matata!

TOM ALAN ROBBINS (*Pumbaa*) Broadway: original companies of *Jerome Robbins' Broadway, Threepenny Opera* (with Sting), *Sunset Boulevard,* and *Once Upon a Mattress.* National Tour: *Les Misérables* (Thernardier). Off-Broadway: *On the Verge, Isn't It Romantic, The Rise and Rise of Daniel Rocket, The Cradle Will Rock.* Television: "Seinfeld," "NYPD Blue," "A Different World," "Murder She Wrote," "Down the Shore." Series regular—"Baby Talk." Alumnus—The Acting Company. Graduate—Juilliard.

JASON RAIZE (*Simba*) recently succeeded Styx singer Dennis DeYoung on the hit national tour of *Jesus Christ Superstar* as Pontius Pilate alongside Ted Neeley and Carl Anderson. Credits include: award-winning productions of *The King and I*, *Miss Saigon*, Yeston-Kopit's *Phantom* (title role) and *Gypsy* (Tulsa). "You will find rest from vain fancies if you perform every act in life as though it were your last."—Marcus Antonius

HEATHER HEADLEY (*Nala*) is overjoyed to be making her Broadway debut with this phenomenal company. Before entering the Pridelands, Heather, a Northwestern alumna, understudied and performed the role of Sarah in the musical *Ragtime*. Heather's credits include leading roles in: *Pippin*, *Dreamgirls*, and *The World Goes 'Round*. Heather wishes to thank her "Mommy" for continued support. She also thanks God for His many blessings—especially this one!

STANLEY WAYNE MATHIS (*Banzai*) Broadway: Jack the Bear in George C. Wolfe's *Jelly's Last Jam*; David Merrick's *Oh, Kay!* Off-Broadway: *Antigone*, Ubu Repertory; *Fantasma*, Public Theater. Regional: *Abyssinia*, Arena Stage, Washington, DC; *Anything Goes*, Theatrefest, Montclair, NJ; *Hot Mikado*, Theater Under the Stars, Houston, TX; *Spunk* and *Day of Absence*, Centerstage, Baltimore, MD; Emily Mann's *Greensboro*, McCarter Theatre, NJ; Randy Newman's *Faust*, Goodman Theatre, Chicago.

TRACY NICOLE CHAPMAN (*Shenzi*) *The Lion King* marks Tracy's fourth Broadway show. Performances include original casts of *The Life* and *The Who's Tommy*. Also on Broadway in *How to Succeed in Business...* Off-Broadway: *The Princess and the Black-Eyed Pea*. First National Tours: *Jelly's Last Jam* and *Once on This Island*. Tracy also writes and plays guitar. She would like to thank God, her family, and friends for their support.

KEVIN CAHOON (*Ed*) A graduate of NYU's Tisch School, Kevin went on to the Broadway production of *The Who's Tommy*. This year, Kevin has been seen in Adrianne Shelly's feature *Sudden Manhattan* and as Kermit Jones on AMC's *The Royale*. Numerous regional credits include Sydney in Anthony Newley's *Chaplin* and Gus in Garland Wright's *Babes in Arms* at the Guthrie. Kevin was also the first Teen Male Vocalist Grand Champion on "Star Search."

SCOTT IRBY-RANNIAR (*Young Simba*) was last seen in the Washington, D.C. production of Andrew Lloyd Webber's *Whistle Down the Wind*. Professional credits include the Disney reading of *Aïda* and Young Clint in *Comfortable Shoes* at the Paper Mill Playhouse. Scott is a student at Manhattan East and Harbor Performing Arts. Scott wishes to thank Mother, Papo, Todd, Milton, Dale, Bertin, and Barry Kolker at FiFi Oscard. I love you Mommy.

KAJUANA SHUFORD (*Young Nala*) is thrilled to be making her Broadway debut in *The Lion King*. Credits include various productions at the Ujama Black Theatre and *Children of Eden* for the National Alliance of Musical Theatres. She has appeared in commercials for Sears and Pillsbury. When not performing, Kajuana enjoys reading and listening to spiritual music. Kajuana would like to thank her mother for all her love and support.

KEVIN BAILEY (*u/s Scar*) Broadway debut. Off-Broadway: *A Midsummer Night's Dream* (Demetrius), *An Unfinished Song* (Worth); National Tours: *The Fantasticks* (El Gallo), *Phantom of the Opera*/Hill version (Phantom), *Jesus Christ Superstar* (Pilate), *The Foreigner* (David Lee). Regional: *Falsettos* (Whizzer), *Guys and Dolls* (Sky Masterson).

EUGENE BARRY-HILL (*Ensemble*) recently completed the national tour of *Ain't Misbehavin'* starring the Pointer Sisters. He also spent five years touring the world as a member of the Grammy-winning group The Fifth Dimension.

GINA BREEDLOVE (*Sarabi, Ensemble*) is a recently signed recording artist with Qwest Records, and has a song on the *Steel* soundtrack. Stage credits include *Sheila's Day*, *If These Shoes Could Talk*, and four international tours with Harry Belafonte. Peace!

CAMILLE M. BROWN (*Ensemble*) Broadway: 1996 award-winning revival of *The King and I*. Concert: formerly Martha Graham Dance Company, soloist. Printwork: Lois Greenfield's *Aireborn*, *Heart & Soul*, *Mirabella*.

IRESOL CARDONA (*Ensemble*) a Nuyorican (NY–Puerto Rican). Trained at LaGuardia H.S., Joffrey, Alvin Ailey, Madame Darvash, Kevin Jeff. Performed with Jubilation!, Joseph Holmes, Deeply Rooted, and Cecilia Marta Co. Mom, Iega, your love supported my first steps.

ALBERTO CRUZ, Jr. (*u/s Young Simba*) has performed in vocal concerts at Madison Square Garden and on the "Kenny Rogers Christmas Show" for four consecutive years. He would like to send his love to his Mom and Dad.

MARK ALLAN DAVIS (*Ensemble*) Broadway debut. Danced with Bill T. Jones/ Arnie Zane, Jose Limon, Peter Goss (Paris), and Impulse Dance Companies. Eleven years in Europe appearing in stage, film, and television productions. Other credits: Opera Jonglage and *Antigone* (Berlin).

LINDIWE DLAMINI (*Swing*) *Sarafina* (Broadway and National Tour). Performances: Radio City Music Hall, *Pocahontas* in Central Park, Grover Washington, "Arsenio," David Letterman, Jay Leno, 1988 Tony Awards, and Essence Awards.

NTOMB'KHONA DLAMINI (*Ensemble*) *Sarafina* (Magundane)— Broadway and National Tour; *Godspell*; *Excuse-Moi*. Performances/soundtracks: *Power of One*, Grover Washington's "Soul Strut," Jay Leno, "Arsenio," Essence Awards '96, David Letterman, Tony Awards, Africare, U.N. Commercials: Reebok, Coca-Cola.

SHEILA GIBBS (*Ensemble*) NYU graduate. Broadway: Mama Euralie in *Once on This Island*; Mocha in *Runaways*; Lucetta in *Two Gentlemen of Verona*. Regional: Lena Younger in *A Raisin in the Sun*; Lady in *Blues in the Night*; Jenny in *Quilters*; Mary in *Elmer Gantry*.

LANA GORDON (*Ensemble*) is excited to make her Broadway debut. Other roles include The Acid Queen in the Gateway Production of *Tommy* and Dionne in the European Tour of *Hair*. She thanks her parents for their love and support.

LINDIWE HLENGWA (*Ensemble*) *Sarafina* (Broadway/National Tour). Soundtracks/Performances: *The Lion King*, *Power of One*, *Rhythm of the Pride Lands*, *Dry White Season*, Michael Bolton, Buster Poindexter video, Ziggy Marley, Arsenio Hall, Hugh Masekela. I thank God for the talent.

TIMOTHY HUNTER (*Ensemble*) returns to Broadway having performed in *Cats*, *Sarafina*, and *Dreamgirls*. Tim has also danced with Anti-Gravity, the Essence Awards, Radio City, and various commercials. Thanks family and friends for love and support.

CHRISTOPHER JACKSON (*Ensemble*) is happy to be making his Broadway debut. He is a graduate of AMDA. Off-Broadway: *Time and the Wind, Bobo's*. He thanks God, his mother, the Take One Co., and family and friends.

JENNIFER JOSEPHS (*u/s Young Nala*) is making her Broadway debut. She has appeared in over 100 print ads and commercials. She is represented by Schuller Talent in NY. Born and raised in Brooklyn, she loves to sing, dance, and act.

VANESSA A. JONES (*Ensemble*) Praise be to God from whom my blessings flow. Broadway/Off-Broadway: *Juan Darién, Buddy, Tapestry, Elmer Gantry*. National Tours: *Jesus Christ Superstar, Hair*. Thanks Mom, Dad, Michelle, Amanda, Nani/ Saperstein, family, and friends.

MICHAEL JOY (*Ensemble*) Broadway debut. Former principal—Alvin Ailey American Dance Theater; he has also appeared in several television, film, and theater productions. Michael thanks his parents for their unconditional love and support and lovingly remembers choreographer Talley Beatty.

FACA KULU (*Ensemble*) Film: *Sarafina, The Ghost and the Darkness*. Vita Award nominee (South Africa). Off-Broadway: *Township Fever, Sacrifices of Mabatho*. Co-wrote and directed musical *Bus Stop Blues*.

RON KUNENE (*Ensemble*) PhD candidate (UCLA). Performances/Soundtracks: *Ace Ventura II, Congo, Sarafina, Listen Up* (Quincy Jones' documentary), *Bopha*, 1995 and 1988 Oscars (*The Lion King* & *Cry Freedom*). Consultant on audio book *Long Walk to Freedom* by Nelson Mandela.

SONYA LESLIE (*Swing*) Making her Broadway debut, Sonya would like to thank God for this wonderful opportunity. Past credits include: *A Chorus Line, Mule Bone*, and *Twelfth Night*. Much love to her family for their love and support.

AUBREY LYNCH II (*Ensemble, Dance Captain*) is a former principal with the Alvin Ailey American Dance Theater. He currently works extensively in print, film, and television and is owner and designer of a line of hand-crocheted, one-of-a-kind wearable art—Aubrey Designs.

PHILIP DORIAN McADOO (*Ensemble*) Broadway debut. For my grandmother; remembering your smile, your laugh, your wisdom. Thanks Jack Waddel (voice teacher) and Taye Diggs for your examples. Mom, my rock. Dad, my hero. Ershlena, my heart—I love you!

SAM McKELTON (*Ensemble*) Broadway debut. Recently starred in *Five Guys...* (Off-Broadway). Opera experience includes *Scourge of Hyacinths* (Munich), *Outcasts* (BAM), and others. Belafonte World Tour—featured artist ('93, '95, '96). Dedicates performances to God, family, and supporters.

PETER ANTHONY MOORE (*Swing*) from Brownsville, NY. A "Fame" High School graduate. Sole recipient of the Playbill Award presented by Clive Barnes. Thanks to my Pastor, Rev. Johny Ray Youngblood, and Adrianne Brown, my first dance teacher.

NANDI MORAKE (*Ensemble*) *Sarafina* (Broadway and National Tour). Performances/Soundtracks: *The Lion King, Pocahontas*, 1988 Tony Awards, 1995 Academy Awards, *Outbreak*, *Ace Ventura*, *Congo*, "Arsenio," NARM Convention, and Miriam Makeba.

NHLANHLA NGEMA (*Ensemble*), a South African, played Stimela in *Sarafina* (Broadway, national tour, and movie). Also appeared in many musicals, touring the world as an actor, singer, dancer. Tony Awards, 1988.

KARINE PLANTADIT-BAGEOT (*Ensemble*) Aubusson, France. Has spent the last seven years as a leading dancer with the Alvin Ailey Dance Theater. Enthusiastically, she makes her musical debut in this Broadway premiere.

DANNY RUTIGLIANO (*u/s Zazu, Timon, Pumbaa*) National Tour: *How To Succeed...* Broadway: *The Best Little Whorehouse Goes Public* (Ralph J. Bostick). Other NYC: *One Touch of Venus* (*Encores!* series), *Topper*, *Godspell, That's Life, Yiddle with a Fiddle*. Many regional appearances. Danny lives in New Jersey with his beautiful wife and best friend, Jacqueline Monroe.

LEVENSKY SMITH (*Ensemble*) Youngstown, Ohio. Credits include: *Cats* (on Broadway). *Fame* (the European Tour), Joseph Holmes Chicago Dance, and Gus Gordano Jazz Dance Chicago. All praises to God for my many blessings.

ASHI K. SMYTHE (*Ensemble*) A host of accomplishments. Appreciates the gift of dance the Lord has given me, and my mother for showing and telling me the things I could accomplish. Thanks Bradley, Karen, and Lendo.

ENDALYN TAYLOR-SHELLMAN (*Ensemble*) Principal with Dance Theatre of Harlem. Member of the Tony Award–winning Broadway production, *Carousel*. TV credits: American Express commercial, PBS' "Great Performances," and NBC special "Giselle," hosted by Bill Cosby. Love to my family.

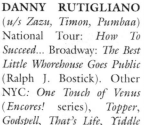

RACHEL TECORA TUCKER (*Swing*) Credits include National Tour of *The Wiz*, Radio City Music Hall Rockette, and Dayton Contemporary Dance Co. Performance dedicated in the memory of Rodney Elijah Tucker.

FRANK WRIGHT II (*Swing*) was last seen in *Miss Saigon* on Broadway. Other credits include: Jim in *Big River*, Thami, and *My Children, My Africa*. He thanks God.

CHRISTINE YASUNAGA (*Ensemble*) Born in Hawaii. B.A. from UCLA. Last seen on Broadway as Topsy in *The King and I*, Radio City's Spring Spectacular, Lula Washington Dance Theatre, and The Hawaii Ballet Theatre. Mahalo for believing in me.

ELTON JOHN (*Music*) Academy Award–winning recording artist, Elton John, released a new studio album in September, 1997, titled *The Big Picture*. The release of this album is especially noteworthy because it also marks the 30th anniversary of one of the most prolific songwriting teams in the history of pop music, Elton John and lyricist Bernie Taupin. Several years ago, Elton John embarked on another noteworthy songwriting collaboration with renowned lyricist, Tim Rice, and this resulted in the tremendously successful soundtrack to the Walt Disney Pictures smash hit, *The Lion King*. The album produced two top-selling, award-winning singles for Elton, "Can You Feel the Love Tonight" and "Circle of Life." To date, the record has surpassed the 10 million mark in sales. The success of *The Lion King* has resulted in yet another Elton John/Tim Rice collaboration. The duo have written new material based on the story depicted in Verdi's classic opera *Aïda* for an upcoming Disney theatrical project. Apart from his musical projects, Elton John continues to be per-sonally involved in the fundraising activities for the Elton John AIDS Foundation which funds direct care services for men, women, and children living with HIV and AIDS. Since it's inception in 1992, the Foundation has distributed more than $13 million in grants worldwide. In addition, as a result of his contributions to charity and the arts, last year, Elton John was added to Queen Elizabeth's Honors List, receiving the prestigious British title of Commander of the Order of the British Empire. This year, in honor of his 50th birthday, he was awarded an Honorary Membership to the Royal Academy of Music in London—a school he attended in his junior years.

TIM RICE (*Lyrics*) Theater: *Joseph and the Amazing Technicolor Dreamcoat*; *Jesus Christ Superstar*; *Evita*; *Blondel*; *Chess*; *Starmania/ Tycoon*; some of *Beauty and the Beast*; *Heathcliff*; *King David*. In the works: *Aïda*. TV/Films: *Three More Men in a Boat*; some of *Aladdin*; *The Lion King*. In the works: *El Dorado*; *The Pheasant That Died of Old Age*. Books: *Evita*; *Treasures of Lord's*; over 30 Guinness Books on British pop music; 22 *Heartaches Cricketers' Almanacks*. In the works: An autobiography.

ROGER ALLERS (*Book*) makes his Broadway debut with this adaptation from the animated feature which he co-directed. Roger has been instrumental in shaping the structure and dialogue for all of the Disney animated features beginning with *Oliver & Company* in 1988. He is currently writing and directing *Kingdom of the Sun*, a Disney Animation feature scheduled for release in 1999. From childhood, Roger has been passionately interested in the art of animation. Prior to working with Disney, he created animation on such diverse programs and films such as "Sesame Street," "The Electric Company," "Make a Wish," "Animalympics," *Tron* and *Little Nemo*. He resides in Venice, California, with his wife, Leslee, and their two children, Leah and Aidan.

IRENE MECCHI (*Book*) began her association with Disney in March, 1992, when she wrote *Recycle Rex*, an animated short which won the 1994 Environmental Media Award. Irene is a co-writer of Disney's animated features *The Lion King*, *The Hunchback of Notre*

Dame, and *Hercules*, and is presently working on Disney's upcoming *Kingdom of the Sun*. A native San Franciscan, Irene is a graduate of the University of California at Berkeley and furthered her theater training at the American Conservatory Theater in San Francisco. Irene has written for print, television, live-action film, as well as a stage play drawn from the 60 years of newspaper columns by San Francisco's Pulitzer Prize–winning writer, Herb Caen.

JULIE TAYMOR (*Director, Costume Designer, Mask/Puppet Co-Designer, Additional Music & Lyrics*) directs theater, opera, and film. She made her Broadway debut in 1996 with her production of *Juan Darién* (Lincoln Center's Vivian Beaumont Theater), which was nominated for five 1997 Tony Awards. Other theater work includes: *The Green Bird* (New Victory Theater and La Jolla Playhouse); *Titus Andronicus*, *The Tempest*, and *The Taming of the Shrew* (Theatre for a New Audience); *Juan Darién* (Music-Theatre Group); co-adapter and director of *Transposed Heads* (Lincoln Center and American Music Theatre Festival) and *Liberty's Taken* (Castle Hill Festival); designer and choreographer of *The King Stag* (American Repertory Theatre). Opera direction: *The Magic Flute* (Maggio Musicale, Florence); *Oedipus Rex* (Saito Kinen Festival, Japan); *Salomé* (Kirov Opera); *The Flying Dutchman* (Los Angeles Opera). Film: *Fool's Fire*, an adaptation of Edgar Allan Poe's *Hopfrog* for American Playhouse. She is currently preparing to direct a feature film of her adaptation of *Titus Andronicus*. Ms. Taymor's awards include a MacArthur Foundation Fellowship, a Guggenheim Fellowship, an Emmy for *Oedipus Rex*, Obie awards for Visual Magic and for *Juan Darién*, the Brandeis Creative Arts Award, the Dorothy Chandler Performing Arts Award, and the International Classical Music Award for Best Opera Production (*Oedipus Rex*). *Playing with Fire*, a book spanning 20 years of Julie Taymor's work, was recently published by Abrams.

GARTH FAGAN (*Choreographer*) For 25 years, Garth Fagan has toured the world with Garth Fagan Dance. On television, the Company has appeared on "Great Performances," "The Tonight Show," and the Academy Awards. Mr. Fagan forged his own dance language and technique drawing from modern dance, Afro-Caribbean, and ballet. Mr. Fagan has choreographed for Alvin Ailey Dance Theatre, Dance Theatre of Harlem, the Jose Limon Company, and others. He directed and choreographed Duke Ellington's *Queenie Pie* at the Kennedy Center and Joseph Papp's *A Midsummer Night's Dream*. A Distinguished University Professor at SUNY Brockport, he has received numerous awards and fellowships including a *Dance Magazine* Award, Guggenheim Fellowship, and Fulbright 50th Anniversary Distinguished Fellowship.

LEBO M (*Additional Music & Lyrics, Additional Vocal Score, Vocal Arrangements, Choral Director, Ensemble*) is known as the "voice and spirit of *The Lion King*." A native of South Africa, his pursuit of a musical career in the U.S. eventually landed him a Grammy for his arrangements of the Disney score in 1994. Lebo was the only African contributor to the smash film, which led to his work on the follow-up album *Rhythm of the Pride Lands*. Schooled at the Duke Ellington School of Music (Washington, D.C.) and the Los Angeles City College Music Department, Lebo was inspired by his native Zulu music, American jazz, and R&B. Credits include: *The Power of One* (co-wrote the music and lyrics, co-produced the soundtrack, and conducted a 110-person choir); *Back on the Block* and *Listen Up* with Quincy Jones; and the feature films *Outbreak* (Warner Bros.), *Congo* (Warner Bros.), and *Born to Be Wild* (Paramount), and the Disney TV special "People." His new album, *Deeper Meaning*, will be released later this year.

MARK MANCINA (*Additional Music & Lyrics, Music Produced for the Stage, Additional Score*) an award-winning composer, was an obvious choice to compose, produce, and adapt additional music for *The Lion King* stage production as he arranged and produced songs for the blockbuster animated feature film, for which he received both the Grammy and American Music Award in 1994. The film also spawned the hit album *Rhythm of the Pride Lands*, for which Mancina co-wrote, arranged, and produced three tracks, including "He Lives in You" and "Shadowland," which are featured in the stage production. Ranked among the upper echelons of film composers, his credits include mega-hits *Speed*, *Twister*, and *Bad Boys*, the period epic *Moll Flanders*, which was on *Billboard's* Classical Crossover Chart, and this summer's hit action thriller *Con Air*, among others. He is recording an album of original material and also plans to embark on a tour featuring musical highlights from his film scores.

HANS ZIMMER (*Additional Music & Lyrics*) received an Oscar, Golden Globe, and two Grammy awards for his film score of *The Lion King*. His long line of over 60 film and TV scores goes back to 1982's "Moonlighting," directed by Jerzy Skolimowski, and includes the Oscar-nominated scores for *The Preacher's Wife* and *Rain Man*, as well as the Grammy Award–winning *Crimson Tide*, *Black Rain*, *Thelma and Louise*, *Driving Miss Daisy*, *Backdraft*, *Green Card*, *Beyond Rangoon*, and *Broken Arrow*. In addition to his composing duties, he has assumed the responsibility of heading DreamWorks' entire film music division, and has scored their first film, *The Peacemaker* starring George Clooney and Nicole Kidman.

JAY RIFKIN (*Additional Music & Lyrics*) The Grammy Award–winning producer, together with producing/composing partner Hans Zimmer, created Media Ventures, a film scoring studio and composer's cooperative. Their partnership has earned them Academy Award nominations for the film scores of *Driving Miss Daisy*, *Rain Man*, and *The Lion King*. Based on the success of *The Lion King* soundtrack, Jay produced the gold-selling follow-up album *Rhythm of the Pride Lands*. He is also the founder and president of Mojo Records, an alternative music label he formed in 1995, home of Goldfinger and Reel Big Fish.

RICHARD HUDSON (*Scenic Design*) was born in Zimbabwe and educated in Zimbabwe and England. He attended the Wimbledon School of Art. He has designed sets and costumes for opera and theater companies all over the world, including The Royal National Theatre, The Royal Shakespeare Company,

Glyndebourne Festival Opera, the Old Vic, The Royal Opera House Covent Garden, and English National Opera (UK), The Bavarian State Opera (Munich), La Fenice (Venice), and Staatsoper (Vienna). In America, he has designed *Twelfth Night* (Goodman Theatre), *The Rake's Progress* (Lyric Opera of Chicago), and *La Bête* (Eugene O'Neill Theatre, NYC). He has won many awards and was recently appointed British Scenography Commissioner to the Originasation Internationale des Scenografes, Techniciens et Architects de Thèatre (OISTAT).

DONALD HOLDER (*Lighting Design*) Broadway: *Juan Darién* (Drama Desk and Tony nominations), *Hughie*, *Eastern Standard*, *Holiday*, *Solitary Confinement*. Off-Broadway credits include: *All My Sons* (Roundabout), *Sight Unseen*, *Three Days of Rain*, *After-Play* (MTC), *The Caucasian Chalk Circle* (Drama Desk nomination) and *Spunk* (NYSF), *Titus Andronicus*, *The Green Bird*, *The Changling* (TFANA) *Fit to Be Tied*, *Avenue X* (Playwrights Horizons), *Jeffrey* (WPA), *The Good Times Are Killing Me* (Second Stage), and *Pterodactyls* (Vineyard). Opera: *Salome* (Kirov Opera, St. Petersburg, Russia). He has designed at resident theaters across the U.S., and his recent architectural lighting projects include Sony Plaza and the Swiss Center in New York. Mr. Holder is a graduate of the Yale School of Drama.

MICHAEL CURRY (*Mask and Puppet Co-Designer*) has collaborated with Julie Taymor on the PBS/American Playhouse film *Fool's Fire*, the opera *Oedipus Rex* conducted by Seiji Ozawa at the Saito Kinen Festival in Japan, and the opera *Die Zauberflöte* at the Maggio Musicale in Florence, Italy. On Broadway, he has worked on numerous shows including *Crazy For You* and *Kiss of the Spider Woman*. He is one of the country's leading puppet consultants and works widely in both conceptual and technical development for some of the world's foremost entertainment companies. He owns and operates Michael Curry Design and Sculptural Engineering in St. Helens, OR, which produces large, live-performance oriented puppets such as those seen at the 1996 Olympic Opening Ceremonies and the Disney theme parks.

TONY MEOLA (*Sound Design*) Broadway includes: *Juan Darién, The Last Night of Ballyhoo, Steel Pier, Forum, The King and I, Company, Moon over Buffalo, Smokey Joe's Cafe, Anything Goes, Face Value, Guys and Dolls, Chronicle of a Death Foretold, A Month in the Country, A Christmas Carol, Five Guys Named Moe, She Loves Me, Whorehouse Goes Public, The Red Shoes, A Grand Night for Singing*. West End: *Smokey Joe's Cafe, Anything Goes*. National Tours include: *Driving Miss Daisy*. Off-Broadway includes: *Violet, Dark Rapture, Durang, Durang, Peccadillo, Groucho, Butterfly* (Goodspeed); *One Man Band, Positive Me*.

MICHAEL WARD (*Hair & Makeup Design*) travels widely with his work. He lives and gardens in London and the Loire Valley, France. Opera credits include *The Rake's Progress* (Chicago and Japan), Richard Jones' much traveled production of *The Love for Three Oranges*. Theater: *Cabaret* and *Joseph...* (West End). Film: Buddy's hair for *Buddy* and *Nightmare*.

JAY BINDER (*Casting*) with associates Jack Bowdan, Mark Brandon, and Amy Kitts. Broadway: *Triumph of Love, Proposals, The Last Night of Ballyhoo, Chicago, Once Upon a Mattress, The King and I, Juan Darién, King David, Damn Yankees, Beauty and the Beast, Laughter on the 23rd Floor, Lost in Yonkers, Jerome Robbins' Broadway, Jake's Women, The Goodbye Girl, Rumors*. Off-Broadway: *Molly Sweeney, London Suite*. *Encores!* Great American Musicals in Concert—four seasons. East Coast casting for Warner Brothers Television (1991–96), "I'll Fly Away," and "New York News." Three time Artios Award winner. Member—Casting Society of America.

DAVID BENKEN (*Technical Director*) makes his Broadway debut with *The Lion King*. He has over 20 years of experience with touring Broadway productions. He is currently the technical supervisor for the national tour of *Miss Saigon*. National tours: *Les Misérables, Carousel, 42nd Street, Evita*, and *Annie*. Other shows: *Evita* (S. Amer.), *West Side Story* (Vienna), *Brigadoon, Oklahoma, Show Boat*. Special thanks and love to his wife Rose Palombo. He would also like to acknowledge the invaluable assistance of Stephen Detmer and Richard Howard.

JEFF LEE (*Production Stage Manager*) as Production Stage Manager/Supervisor— Broadway & touring: *A Chorus Line, Cats, Ain't Misbehavin', Pirates of Penzance, Joseph..., Merlin, Juan Darién, Hapgood, The Little Foxes*; as Director—national & international: *Shirley Valentine, Cats, Joseph..., Song of Singapore, Love Julie, Mortal Kombat*. Thanks Silvita.

JOSEPH CHURCH (*Music Director*) credits as music director include Randy Newman's *Faust* in San Diego and Chicago, *The Who's Tommy* on Broadway (also music supervisor of all worldwide companies), Radio City's Christmas Spectacular and *Little Shop of Horrors* (national tour). His work as a composer includes incidental music for over 30 plays and two Off-Broadway musicals. He is currently collaborating with librettist Sheldon Harnick on an oratorio, *Les Fables*. Mr. Church holds a doctorate from NYU, where he is co-director of the music theater program and teaches composition.

ROBERT ELHAI (*Associate Music Producer, Orchestrator*) His debut as a Broadway orchestrator follows many years of orchestrating theater and film scores for renowned composers Elliot Goldenthal (*Juan Darién, Othello, Interview with the Vampire*) and Michael Kamen (*101 Dalmatians, Don Juan De Marco*), among others. He holds a doctorate in composition from Yale University and currently resides in Minneapolis.

DAVID METZGER (*Orchestrator*) makes his Broadway debut with this production. He has previously worked as an orchestrator on many films, including *Speed 2*. He has arranged or composed over 250 pieces for "The Tonight Show" with Jay Leno, and worked on numerous national television commercials. David currently resides in Oregon.

BRUCE FOWLER (*Orchestrator*) is an accomplished musician who has composed pieces for such dance companies as the L.A. Chamber Ballet and The Repitoire Dance Theatre. In addition to performing on several film/TV soundtracks, he was the orchestrator for such hit films as *The Lion King, The Rock, Crimson Tide, Backdraft, Twister, The Preacher's Wife, Speed*, and *Con Air*. Recently he orchestrated the score for the DreamWorks film *The Peacemaker*.

MICHAEL KELLER (*Music Coordinator*) has drummed in numerous Broadway shows as well as for Dionne Warwick, The Fifth Dimension, Rodney Dangerfield, and The Manhattan Rhythm Kings; currently he is both drummer and conductor for Marvin Hamlisch in concert. Music Coordination: *The Goodbye Girl* (1993); *Barbara Streisand—The Concert* (1994); *The Music of Andrew Lloyd Webber* (1995); *Whistle Down the Wind* (1996).

KARL JURMAN (*Associate Conductor*) Broadway: Associate Musical Supervisor International/Conductor—*Beauty and the Beast, Guys and Dolls, Will Rogers Follies, Into the Woods*. Musical direction: *Whorehouse Goes Public, Lies & Legends/Harry Chapin* (Off-Broadway). Karl would love to thank his wife, actress Mary D'Arcy.

CHRIS MONTAN (*Executive Music Producer*) joined Disney in 1984, and is currently serving as the executive producer of feature animation music, producing motion pictures and television specials for the Studio as well as providing consultation on music-related projects. Under his guidance as head of music, soundtracks from seven theatrical releases (*Cocktail, Beaches, The Little Mermaid, Pretty Woman, Beauty and the Beast, Aladdin*, and *The Lion King*) were certified multi-platinum. Additionally, the Studio received Grammy, Golden Globe, and Academy Award recognition for many of its music entries. Most recently he was the executive music producer on the music for *Pocahontas, Toy Story, The Hunchback of Notre Dame*, and *Hercules*. His company's current projects include a new all-star television production of Rodgers and Hammerstein's classic *Cinderella* for ABC.

WALT DISNEY THEATRICAL PRODUCTIONS (*Producer*) a division of The Walt Disney Company, operates under the direction of Peter Schneider and Thomas Schumacher. Disney's inaugural production, the Tony Award–winning *Beauty and the Beast*, continues in its fourth year on Broadway and is currently being performed in Chicago, London, Tokyo, Fukuoka, Mexico City, and Stuttgart (opening in December). The Disney Company completed restoration of the historic New Amsterdam Theatre on 42nd Street this past May, opening with a concert version of Alan Menken and Tim Rice's *King David*. Future plans include a new musical by Elton John and Tim Rice based on the story of Aida.

Walt Disney Theatrical Productions

President	Peter Schneider
Executive Vice President	Thomas Schumacher
Creative Affairs	Stuart Oken
General Manager	Alan Levey
Production Supervisors	John De Santis, Bob Routolo, John Tiggeloven
Business Affairs	Kevin Breen, Gabrielle Klatsky, Harry Gold, Robbin Kelley, Karen Lewis, Dan Posener
Labor Relations	John Petrafesa, Sr., Robert W. Johnson, Leslie Ann Bennett
Marketing	Ron Kollen, Deb Axtell, Frank Conway, Jack Eldon, Kim First
International	Skip Malone
Finance	Clark Spencer, Amy Copeland, Shimanti Guha, David Schrader, Alan Guno, Steven Klein, Scott Savoie, Ron Villarreal
Development	Alice Jankell, Michelle Mindlin, Michael Sanfilippo
Group Sales	Chip Brown, Leslie Case, Tami Carlson
Administrative Staff	Elliot Altman, Jane T.N. Collins, Carl Flanigan, Jay Hollenback, Debbie Hoy, Stacie Iverson, Connie Jasper, Risa Kelly, Aaron Levin, Diane Mellen, Patti Mills, Mary Ann Parsons, Mary Lou Pawley, Danielle Pinnt, Roberta Risafi, Robyn Ruehl, Andy Temesvary, Susan Tyker, Marianne Virtuoso, Derek Wadlington, Pam Waterman, Julianna Wineland

Staff for *The Lion King*

Associate Producer . . . . Donald Frantz
Project Manager . . . . Nina Essman

**GENERAL PRESS REPRESENTATIVES
BONEAU/BRYAN-BROWN**
Chris Boneau • Patty Onagan • Jackie Green
Miguel Tuason • Joel Hile

Company Manager . . . . . STEVEN CHAIKELSON
Assistant Company Manager . . . . .Johanna Pfaelzer
Stage Manager . . . . Mahlon Kruse
Stage Manager . . . . .Elizabeth Burgess
Stage Manager . . . . Steve 'Doc' Zorthian
Assistant Directors . . . .Dan Fields, Michele Steckler
Assistant Choreographer . . . .Norwood J. Pennewell,
Natalie Rogers
Dance Captain . . . . Aubrey Lynch II
Assistant Dance Captain . . . . Rachel Tecora Tucker
Management Associate . . . . Nick Lobel-Weiss

Associate Scenic Designers . . . . Peter Eastman,
Jonathan Fensom
Scenic Design Assistants . . . . . . Catherine Chung,
David Cozier, Sarah Eckert,
Michael Fagin, Paul Kelly,
Hyun-Joo-Kim, Mark Nayden,
Steve Olson, Atkin Pace,
Russell Parkman, Dawn Petrlik
Associate Lighting Designer . Jeanne Koenig Rubin
Assistant Lighting Designer . . . . . . .Martin Vreeland
Lighting Design Assistant . . . . .Karen Spahn
Projection Designer . . . . .Geoff Puckett
Projection Art . . . . .Caterina Bertolotto
Assistant Sound Designer . . . . .Kai Harada
Associate Costume
Designer . . . . .Mary Nemecek Peterson
Assistant Costume Designer . . . . . . .Tracy Dorman
Costume Design Assistants . . . . Kristian Kraai,
Marion Williams
Mask/Puppet Studio Dept. Heads . . . Pete Beeman,
Loren Bevans, Sue Bonde,
Jeff Curry, Liza Pastine,
Mark Spivey, Debra Temenbaum
Mask/Puppet Craftpeople . . . . Emily Bank,
Roi Bobiak, Debra Bruneaux,
Katia Debear, Gary Graham,
Debrah Glassberg, Patricia Gropusso,
Paul Jenkins, Brett Kahler,
Steven Kaplan, Maria Klein,
Gabriel Koren, Sky Lanigan,
David Laubenthal, Nelson Lowry,
Mike Marsh, Brad Pace,
Anne Salt, Manju Shandler,
Cyndee Starr, Mari Tobita, Christopher Webb
Design Studio Coordinator . . . . . Jason Scott Eagan

Associate Technical Director . . Stephen M. Detmer
Production Carpenter . . . . Drew Siccardi
Automation . . . . Rick Howard
Assistant
Carpenters . . . . . . .Steven McEntee, Michael Trotto
Automation Carpenters . . . . Steven Stackle,
George Zegarsky

Production Flyman . . . . .Brad Ingram
Production Electrician . . . . James Maloney
Key Spot Operator . . . . Joseph P. Garvey
Board Operator . . . . Edward M. Greenberg
Automated Lighting Technician . . .Sean Strohmeyer
Automated Lighting Programmer . . Aland Henderson
Automated Lighting Tracker . . . . Lara Bohon
Production Propman . . . . .Victor Amerling
Assistant Propman . . . . Baron Becker
Production Sound Engineer . . . . Scott Stauffer
Assistant Sound Engineer . . . .Marie Renée Foucher
Wardrobe Supervisor . . . . .Kjeld Andersen
Assistant Wardrobe Supervisor/
Puppet Master . . . . Louis Troisi
Hair Supervisor . . . . .John "Jack" Curtin
Assistant Hair Supervisor . . . . . . Monte C. Haught
Makeup Supervisor . . . . Kate Chittenden
Assistant Makeup Supervisor . . . . Elizabeth Cohen

Production Assistants . . . . Ryan Baker,
Genoveva Castañeda, Carrie Christensen,
Theresa Gonzales, Hillary Knill, Lisa Koch,
Gabriel Koren, Benjamin Krevolin,
Bev Jensen, Annie McKilligan,
Babette Roberts, Elizabeth Rohr,
Ria Tyriver, Susan Vargo, Justin Wilkes
Production Interns . . . . Bill Augustin,
Ilyse Bosch, Bo Yin Chan,
Carly Dranginis, Michael Duffy,
Christopher Economakos, James Festante,
Ari Glazer, Kimberly Gordon,
Nicole Hudson, Vinny Iaropoli,
Sara Kannenberg, Wayne Knaub,
Matthew Legreca, Maiko Matsushima,
Felicia Pearce, Melissa Ring,
Andrea Sarubbi, Mark E. Smith,
Jennifer Tonnensen, Janine Vanderhoff,
Jacob Williams, Christina Wong
SSDC Observers . . .Caden Manson, Melanie Martin

Executive Music Producer . . . . .Chris Montan
Music Development . . . . .Nick Glennie-Smith
Music Preparation . . . Donald Oliver & Evan Morris
Chelsea Music Service, Inc.
Synthesizer Programmer . . . . .Ted Baker
Orchestral Synthesizer Programmer . .Christopher Ward
Electronic Drum Programmer . . . . .Tommy Igoe
Additional Percussion
Arrangements . . . . .Valerie Dee Naranjo
Music Assistant . . . . .Elizabeth J. Falcone
Personal Assistant to Elton John . . . . . . Bob Halley
Assistant to Tim Rice . . . . Eileen Heinink
Assistant to Mark Mancina . . . . Robbie Boyd

Associate Casting Director . . . . .MARK BRANDON
Casting Associates . . . . .Jack Bowden, Amy Kitts
Casting Assistant . . . . .Laura Stanczyk
Stunt Consultant . . . . .Peter Moore
Physical Therapy . . . . . Sean Gallagher - Performing
Arts Physical Therapy, Inc.
Orthopedist . . . . .Dr. Philip Bauman
Assistant to Associate Producer . . . . Alice A. Farrell
Corporate Counsel . . . . .Michael Rosenfeld
Production Accountants . . Dolores Salkow, Ann Caprio

Banking . . . . .Barbara Von Borstel,
Morgan Guaranty Trust Co.
Children's Tutoring . . . . . . On Location Education
Child Guardian . . . . Dale Kimber
Press Assistants . . . . .Patrick Paris, Alison McDonald
Production Photography . . . . Joan Marcus,
Marc Bryan-Brown
Documentary
Photography/Video . . . . Kenneth Van Sickle
Merchandising . . . . . . .Disney Consumer Products

Disney's *The Lion King* is a registered trademark owned by the Walt Disney Company and used under special license by Walt Disney Theatrical Productions Ltd.
Cover Art Design © Disney.

CREDITS

Scenery built and mechanized by Hudson Scenic Studio, Inc. Additional scenery by Chicago Scenic Studios, Inc., Edge & Co., Inc., Michael Hagen, Inc., Piper Productions, Inc., Scenic Technologies, Inc., I. Weiss & Sons, Inc.; Lighting by Westsun; VARI*LITE® automated lighting provided by Vari-Lite, Inc.; Props by John Creech Design & Production; Sound equipment by Pro-Mix, Inc., additional sound equipment by Walt Disney Imagineering; Rehearsal Scenery by Brooklyn Scenic & Theatrical; Costumes executed by Barbara Matera Ltd., Parsons-Meares Ltd., Donna Langman, Eric Winterling, Danielle Gisiger, Suzie Elder. Millinery by Rodney Gordon, Janet Linville, Arnold Levine. Shibori dyeing by Joan Morris. Custom dyeing and painting by Joni Johns, Mary Macy, Parsons-Meares Ltd., Gene Mignola. Additional Painting by J. Michelle Hill. Knitwear by Maria Ficalora. Footwear by Sharlot Battin, Robert W. Jones, Capezio, Vasilli Shoes. Costume Development by Constance Hoffman. Special Projects by Angela M. Kahler, Patricia Fistes-Adams; custom fabrics developed by Gary Graham and Helen Quinn; Puppet Construction by Michael Curry Design, Inc. and Vee Corporation; Shadow puppetry by Steven Kaplan; *Pumbaa* by Andrew Benepe; Flying by Foy; Trucking by Clark Transfer; Wigs created by Wig Workshop of London, Marimbas by De Morrow Instruments, Ltd., Latin Percussion by LP Music Group, Drumset by Premiere Drums. House Video monitors provided by Mitsubishi Electronics.

SONG EXCERPTS (used by permission)

"Be Our Guest" written by Alan Menken and Howard Ashman; "Five Foot Two, Eyes of Blue" written by Sam Lewis, Joe Young, and Ray Henderson; "The Lion Sleeps Tonight" written by Hugo Peretti, George David Weiss, and Luigi Creatore.

For Group Sales Call: (800) 439-9000
Theater Parties/Special Events (212) 282-2907

Staff for the New Amsterdam Theatre

Theatre Manager . . . . Dana Amendola
Theatre Operations Manager . . . . .Fran Coiro
Box Office Manager . . . . .Jerome Kane
Box Office Treasurer . . . . .Helen Cullen
Guest Relations Manager . . .John M. Loiacono
Administrative Assistant . . . . . . .Alice Acemyan
Chief Engineer . . . . .Frank Gibbons
Engineers . . . . .David Micucci, Tony Sinodinos
Accountant . . . . .Julie Openshaw
Lobby Refreshments . . . . .Sweet Concessions
Special thanks . . . . .Harry Grossman,
Lynn Beckemeyer,
Amy Bawdin, Nancy Holland

WARNING

The photographing or sound recording of any performance or the possession of any device for such photographing or sound recording inside the theatre, without the written permission of the management, is prohibited by law. Violators may be punished by ejection and violations may render the offender liable for money damages.

Latecomers will be seated at the discretion of the management. Patrons with disabilities: wheelchair seating is availible in a variety of theater locations. When ordering your tickets, please indicate any special needs. For our hearing-impaired guests, the theater is equipped with infra-red listening devices; please contact an usher for assistance.

 The actors and stage managers engaged in this production are members of Actors' Equity Association.

 Backstage and Front of the House Employees are represented by the International Alliance of Theatrical Stage Employees (I.A.T.S.E.).

United Scenic Artists represents the designers and scenic painters for the American theatre.

FIRE NOTICE

The exit indicated by a red light and sign nearest to the seat you occupy is the shortest route to the street. In the event of a fire or other emergency please do not run—WALK TO THAT EXIT.

Thoughtless persons annoy patrons and endanger the safety of others by lighting matches or smoking in prohibited areas during the performance and intermissions. This violates a City ordinance and is punishable by law.

FIRE COMMISSIONER